His Delicate Eyes for Her

A Closer Look at the Eternal Father's Love and Concern for Every Woman and Girl

I0154363

Tricia Nicola M.

AB ASPECT Books
www.ASPECTBooks.com

Table of Contents

Introduction 5

Chapter 1: The Promise of a Better
Life Is Real 13

Chapter 2: The Beauty of the
Acceptance. 17

Chapter 3: The Introduction of
Modest Dressing 21

Chapter 4: You Are Courageous 27

Introduction

Are you able to see your lovely value? Do you understand your infinite worth?

The eternal Father has pledged infinite support to you which cannot be severed. Our bodies are considered a "temple" that the eternal Father's Spirit can dwell in. As a result of this we are endowed with special spiritual privileges. These are privileges of honor and power that can take us to very high places throughout our lifetime.

"Then the word of the LORD came unto me, saying, Before I formed thee in the belly I knew thee; and before thou camest forth out of the womb I sanctified thee, and I ordained thee a prophet unto the nations" (Jer. 1:4–5).

The Father of the universe is willing and excited to commune with us through His invisible Holy Spirit which is His power, and our bodies are the medium of that communication, and receptor of that shared power. "Yet to us there is but one God, the Father, of whom are all things, and we unto him; and one Lord Jesus Christ, by whom are all things, and we by him" (1 Cor. 8:6, DRA).

It pleases the Father when we accept the invitation to care for our bodies as a sacred place where His Spirit can dwell.

I beseech you therefore, brethren, by the mercies of God, that ye present your bodies a living sacrifice, holy, acceptable unto God, which is your reasonable service. And be not conformed to this world: but be ye transformed by

the renewing of your mind, that ye may prove what is that good, and acceptable, and perfect, will of God. (Rom. 12:1–2)

When we enter into worship with the eternal Father, and we are reverent in our approach and attire, it shows Him that we love Him, and we accept the gift of friendship with Him as our God and Creator.

The patterns of this world may seem appealing, but we are asked not to be conformed to its pattern. What does that mean? It means we are asked not to follow the styles of everyone or every current trend of clothing and hair-styles, especially if it is not in complete agreement with what our heavenly Father asks us to do. Everything we do should be done to the glory of our eternal Father.

In 1 Corinthians 10:31, it says, "Whether therefore ye eat, or drink, or whatsoever ye do, do all to the glory of God." For example, if we eat excessively without balance, or not enough good nutrients, if we eat and our bodies are being deprived of the right nutrients and we can manage to do better, then we're not eating to the glory of the eternal Father.

One of the reasons to follow this plan is because if we do not implement what God has asked us to, reproach will come to His holy name and our lifestyle and health will reflect a loss.

In 1 Timothy 4:8–9, NIV, it says, "For physical training is of some value, but godliness has value for all things, holding promise for both the present life and the life to come.

This is a trustworthy saying that deserves full acceptance."

A godly lifestyle has the promise of a life that is to come, a good life.

We are very special, and our training is not mere physical, but godliness is the ideal aim. It has a value for all things in this life and the life to come.

You may ask yourself, "What is this godliness? What is the ideal aim? How does it help us?" A godly life is kindness; it is compassion; it is holding back when we feel like cursing at someone, it is volunteering, it is sharing and investing our talents, it is praying and asking the Father for guidance always.

There are times when we have to make sound decisions based on our current situation. 1 Timothy 5:23, says, "Drink no longer water, but use a little wine for thy stomach's sake and thine often infirmities." Timothy had stomach gastrointestinal problems which often made him sick. He was frequently ill, so Paul let him know that some medicine was necessary for the improvement of his condition.

Sometimes we are challenged with illnesses in our bodies and we may have to take medications but let us try to improve our condition and better our health as we are able.

If we are physically challenged because of a disability or because sickness has taken root in our bodies, sometimes pain, whether physically or emotionally, has held our bodies captive, peace and joy is still a gift for us to claim.

"For God hath not given us the spirit of fear; but of power, and of love, and of a sound mind" (2 Tim. 1:7).

We can still exercise our minds to think of positive things, to think of the time when we will walk again, when we will run again, when we will be able to do things without pain again, because this world is temporary.

I want you to know and believe that …

Heaven Is Real
God Is Real
You Are Real

Chapter 1

The Promise of a Better Life Is Real

The Holy Spirit dwells in us. This realization helps us to have privileges of self-discipline, love, power, and enjoyment.

"But they that wait on the LORD shall renew their strength; they shall mount up with wings as eagles; they shall run, and not be weary; and they shall walk, and not faint" (Isa. 40:31).

Here we are reminded that as we accept the eternal Father's Spirit, and we believe and hope in the Father, He will renew our strength.

Though we feel sad, He will renew
Though we feel ashamed, He will renew
Though we feel embarrassed, He will renew
Though we feel broken, He will renew
Though we feel let down, He will renew

Even in trying circumstances, His love is ever so close. There are also times when fear controls our thoughts and actions. It controls our choice of clothing. We want acceptance, we sometimes struggle to find our place, but the eternal Father gives us peace.

Never, never again to feel weary. Not only do we have the Father's love but we have the Son's love. "Let not your heart be troubled. You believe in God, believe also in me [Jesus is speaking here]. In my Father's house there are many mansions" (John 14:1–2, DRA).

There is great courage to be taken from the excerpts of Matthew 6:25–34:

Therefore I say unto you, Take no thought for your life, what ye shall eat, or what ye shall drink; nor yet for your body, what ye shall put on. Is not the life more than meat, and the body than raiment? Behold the fowls of the air: for they sow not, neither do they reap, nor gather into barns; yet your heavenly Father feedeth them. Are ye not much better than they? Which of you by taking thought can add one cubit unto his stature? And why take ye thought for raiment? Consider the lilies of the field, how they grow; they toil not, neither do they spin: And yet I say unto you, That even Solomon in all his glory was not arrayed like one of these. Wherefore, if God so clothe the grass of the field, which to day is, and to morrow is cast into the oven, shall he not much more clothe you, O ye of little faith? Therefore take no thought, saying, What shall we eat? or, What shall we drink? or, Wherewithal shall we be clothed? (For after all these things do the Gentiles seek:) for your heavenly Father knoweth that ye have need of all these things. But seek ye first the kingdom of God, and his righteousness; and all these things shall be added unto you. Take therefore no thought for the morrow: for the morrow shall take thought for the things of itself. Sufficient unto the day is the evil thereof.

Chapter 2
The Beauty of the Acceptance

Once we have accepted the eternal Father's Spirit, we become His and share special privileges. Nothing can separate us from Him or His Son.

For I am sure that neither death nor life, nor angels nor rulers, nor things present nor things to come, nor powers, nor height nor depth, nor anything else in all creation, will be able to separate us from the love of God in Christ Jesus our Lord. (Rom. 8:38–39, ESV)

If we trust the eternal Father, believing that He will see us through, we will see miracles in our lives.

Blessed be the man that trusteth in the Lord, and the Lord shall be his confidence. And he shall be as a tree that is planted by the waters, that spreadeth out its roots towards moisture: and it shall not fear when the heat cometh. And the leaf thereof shall be green, and in the time of drought it shall not be solicitous, neither shall it cease at any time to bring forth fruit. (Jer. 17:7–8, DRA)

"Do not be anxious about anything, but in everything by prayer and supplication with thanksgiving let your requests be made known to God" (Phil. 4:6–8, ESV).

What is it that you are in need of? Clothing, shoes, more money? Whatever it is, trust in

the eternal Father and He will supply all your needs. Just be patient in your asking.

I want you to know this very fact: ***with the eternal Father as our ally, we have a link with the Highest of heaven.***

Chapter 3

The Introduction of Modest Dressing

It was a contractual binding bond that began in the Garden of Eden. When the eternal Father said, "Let there be light" and there was light" (Gen. 1:3, ESV). God saw how good light was, the Father and Son enjoyed the beauty of the light in Their creation. As they continued in

Their creating, the eternal Father said, "Let us make man in our image, after our [kindness] likeness" (Gen. 1:26, ESV). Our Father created us in His image, in the divine image, male and female. He blessed and gave us dominion, power, pride, and joy.

If we remain in His care, doubt and fear will not hold us captive. We have the right to strength and victory.

"And the man and his wife were both naked and were not ashamed" (Gen. 2:25, ESV). When we wander away from our Father's care, fear sets in.

After Eve and her husband sinned, their eyes were now exposed to sin. They saw themselves naked, and they hid themselves. Though they had no physical problems, their decision to disobey created doubt and fear and now they were experiencing this new emotion which made them hide in fear of being seen as naked.

Ever since disobedience led to sin, the human race has been exposed to physical challenges.

Our eyes have not been able to see ourselves or others in the same manner as before the fall.

This drastic change led our heavenly Father to make our first clothing of complete protection.

This clothing was introduced to initiate the *"new need"* for a covering for our physical bodies. "Unto Adam also and to his wife did the LORD God make coats of skins, and clothed them" (Gen. 3:21).

From my research it was the eternal Father who made us aware of the importance of caring for the skin. The integumentary system has needs and He taught us about not wearing materials of mixed types because of the different electrical stimulants it gives which can cause imbalanced charges to our neurological electrical system.

"Thou shalt not wear a garment of divers sorts, as of woollen and linen together" (Deut. 22:11).

The reason for this is because some synthetic fibers can cause dermatitis. It is known that each fiber has a different stimulus and if we are receiving many different stimuli on the body at the same time, it can cause disturbances to our moods, thought patterns, and feelings.

We can note that the clothing of the priest was of specific material and design. Exodus 28:39 says, "And thou shalt embroider the coat of fine linen, and thou shalt make the mitre of fine linen."

Sometimes we cannot control the fabrics we wear, but as we are able, let's first choose natural fiber for optimum benefits. If you are able, avoid blended fabric clothing. I would consider acrylic to be the worst to wear as it causes the most irritation and disruption to your hormonal balance.

What is modesty?

Modesty is temperance and balance in the way we care for our temple, our body. The food we eat—does it help in sustaining us? The clothing we wear—does it call unnecessary attention to us? Is it humble yet lovely? The adornments

we wear—are they humble and not atten-
tion-seeking? Our cosmetic makeup—is it nat-
ural-toned to match our skin type? The music
we listen to—is it uplifting and does it speak of
clean, encouraging words and principles? All
that we do and participate in is fitting us for
our royal legacy with the Son of God.

A POEM

*Constantly upon her, He sees all the pressure of
conformity that assaults her very existence.*

He sees the limited choices that befall her.

*But in the midst of all the madness
and new clothing designs,
His eyes are still supportive and caring.*

*He declares that her holiness is
His most precious possession.*

*As she awaits her love, let her maintain
a purity of dress, let her be ever mindful
of her attire in public places.
Let her wear clothing that properly
covers her sacred parts.*

*Let her long enjoy feminine clothing; these are
gifts of distinction for her.*

*As angels veil their faces when they approach
Him, let her position reverence in ministry on
His behalf, covering her hair, clad simply,
but nice and orderly.*

*His eyes for her are one of unique separateness,
a peculiar people.*

*His eyes for her are delicate, watching to protect
and defend, if only she remains in His care.*

Chapter 4
You Are Courageous

We are asked to be *courageous* in a time when temptation assails us, and things that pull us away from the eternal Father are ever at our fingertips. We know that those things bring sadness and disappointment. We are cautioned to stand firm in our decision to dress modestly and know that this strength builds courage and victory for tomorrow's challenges.

"If thou hast run with the footmen, and they have wearied thee, then how canst thou contend with horses? and if in the land of peace, wherein thou trustedst, they wearied thee, then how wilt thou do in the swelling of Jordan?" (Jer. 12:5).

We are encouraged to remember the eternal Father while we are young, strong, and have good health. Even if we are young and have challenging health concerns, it is still the best time to remember the Creator. "Remember now thy Creator in the days of thy youth" (Eccles. 12:1).

Jeremiah 13:15–16, says, "Hear ye, and give ear; be not proud: for the Lord hath spoken. Give glory to the Lord your God, before he cause darkness, and before your feet stumble upon the dark mountains."

Let us consider that nakedness has been a prideful punishment since the fall of Adam and Eve. "Therefore will I discover thy skirts upon thy face, that thy shame may appear" (Jer. 13:26).

So, we are to wear clothing of modest choice, one that does not draw much attention to self.

In worship, let's praise Him with festal attire, looking nice and joyous, yet modest. Let's be reverent as we approach our heavenly Father in prayer, songs of praise, and prophecies.

Choosing to not let our wardrobe be filled with the worries of the constant change in fashion is a sacrifice, I know, but as we choose to be modest, and cherish our temple, we are honoring the eternal Father. He will give us never-ending joy—joy that is not changing by season, nor does it cost anything.

"Behold, the eye of the Lord is upon them that fear him, upon them that hope in his mercy" (Ps. 33:18).

A rich banquet is awaiting us. With your eternal Father, you can and will overcome anything that bothers you. His love for you is so profound. Let us spend time writing songs of praise to Him, or develop a hobby that builds our character. Remember He has a love for you. His character is full of honesty and justice.

"He loveth righteousness and judgment: the earth is full of the goodness of the Lord" (Ps. 33:5).

Clothes, adornments, and jobs don't define us. And even when we feel out of place, He is right there. "The Lord is nigh unto them that are of a broken heart; and saveth such as be of a contrite spirit" (Ps. 34:18).

Sometimes people don't know how to love you. They don't know your worth. They are not familiar with your unique calling and they give you less than you deserve, but you have to look towards your heavenly King, and reminisce on His love.

He loves you with an everlasting love and it never fails. Leaning too heavily on human love can lead to sadness, even if it is a best friend, parent, caregiver, child, husband, or boyfriend. People can only give what they have. Sometimes, honestly, they don't have much.

So celebrate you. Celebrate your uniqueness from the mighty Creator, and let Him tell you of the redeeming love He has towards you.

No one can ever accurately equate your value. Your price is far above any ruby or even diamonds. Stay your course. Believe in yourself.

Be happy with who you are today and tomorrow. Your glorious personality will continue to develop and the eternal Father will not finish

His marvelous work in you until you become who you were meant to be and He confirms your own uniqueness.

Your only job is to hold on and keep your dependence on the Father. His love is one of dependability. The eternal Father loves us so much that He sent His only begotten Son to rescue us from a world set on damnation. The mighty, ever-powerful Angel of the LORD is the Son of the LORD and He left His lofty position to take on humanity, to save humanity. He was the sacrifice, and He accomplished the greatest link between two individuals, a link between us and the Father.

Nothing can separate us from His love. As the world rushes on, and you find yourself so busy, take a moment and look up at the sunset, taking deep breaths. This creates a relation of peace with yourself. Bask in a moment of fresh air as much as you can, making every effort to do it, you will find yourself lighter in spirits, your anxiety washing away in that moment.

You are a fighter; you are a winner; you can be the bright star the Eternal wants you to be.

There are times when we feel overwhelmed with certain obstacles, but we can safely trust that our heavenly Father knows.

Remember …

You are very lovely and pretty just as you are.

A beautiful variety of colors in the eternal Father's garden of creation—black, pink, orange, brown, mixed colors, a beautiful array of melanin.

Psalms 19:14

"Let the words of my mouth, and the meditation of my heart, be acceptable in thy sight, O Lord, my strength, and my redeemer."

Psalms 34:8–9

"O taste and see that the Lord is good: blessed is the man that trusteth in him. O fear the Lord, ye his saints: for there is no want to them that fear him."

AB ASPECT Books

We invite you to view the complete
selection of titles we publish at:
www.ASPECTBooks.com

We encourage you to write us
with your thoughts about this,
or any other book we publish at:
info@ASPECTBooks.com

ASPECT Books' titles may be purchased in
bulk quantities for educational, fund-raising,
business, or promotional use.
bulksales@ASPECTBooks.com

Finally, if you are interested in seeing
your own book in print, please contact us at:
publishing@ASPECTBooks.com
We are happy to review your manuscript at no charge.

www.ingramcontent.com/pod-product-compliance
Lightning Source LLC
Chambersburg PA
CBHW060810110426
42739CB00032BA/3168